Super
Manipulative
Books

Easy How-to's for 10 Interactive Books That Kids Will Love to Make and Read

by Rozanne Lanczak Williams

NEW YORK • TORONTO • LONDON • AUCKLAND • SYDNEY **Teaching** *Resources*
MEXICO CITY • NEW DELHI • HONG KONG • BUENOS AIRES

To my pals Raquel Herrera, Sue Lewis,
and Barbara Maio. Group hug!
—RLW

The activities in this book have been reviewed for safety and are meant to be done by children with adult supervision and assistance. The author does not assume any responsibility for injuries or accidents that might result from performing these activities without proper supervision.

Cover design, interior design, and interior photos by Josué Castilleja
Cover and interior illustrations by Maxie Chambliss
Assembly illustrations by Jason Robinson

ISBN: 0-439-39504-6
Copyright © 2004 by Rozanne Lanczak Williams
Published by Scholastic Inc.
All rights reserved.
Printed in the U.S.A.

2 3 4 5 6 7 8 9 10   40   11 10 09 08 07 06 05 04

Contents

INTRODUCTION

Dear Teacher,

Welcome to *Super Manipulative Books*! Encourage, inspire, and support the growing literacy skills of your beginning readers with 10 adorable, easy-to-make books. Simply photocopy the reproducible templates and follow the step-by-step directions to assemble these hands-on books— each with its own unique format. You'll find clock hands to turn, flaps to lift, and even ingredients to add to soup! Children personalize the book pages with text and artwork to make the books truly their own.

Enhance your literacy program by including bookmaking activities as part of your classroom routine throughout the school year. Making books with children encourages their interest in writing and helps nurture a lifelong love of reading. After sharing their books at school, young authors will enjoy taking their books home to reread again and again with family members.

Why Make Books?

Bookmaking in the classroom is a great way to
- create age-appropriate books.
- give children practice reading high-frequency words in context.
- introduce children to the steps in the writing process.
- engage children in a meaningful activity during center time or when you are working with small groups.
- integrate reading and writing into the content areas with books that reinforce math skills (*What Time Is It?* and *Frogs on a Log*) and science concepts (*How a Butterfly Grows*).
- create a supply of reading material for children to take home.

Have fun making, reading, and sharing manipulative books!

Rozanne Langh Williams

Rozanne Lanczak Williams

Connections to the Language Arts Standards

The activities in this book support the following language arts standards, outlined by Mid-continent Research for Education and Learning (McREL), a nationally recognized nonprofit organization that collects and synthesizes national and state K–12 standards.

* Uses the stylistic and rhetorical aspects of writing.

* Uses grammatical and mechanical conventions in written compositions.

* Uses the general skills and strategies of the reading process.

Source:
Content Knowledge: A Compendium of Standards and Benchmarks for K–12 Education, 4th edition (Mid-continent Research for Education and Learning)

WHAT'S INSIDE

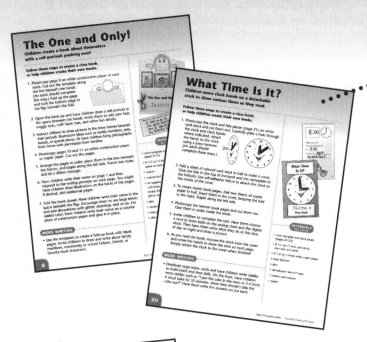

For each manipulative book, you'll find the following:

Directions for the Teacher

This page includes:

- a sample of a completed book cover and an interior page.
- a list of materials.
- easy step-by-step directions for making the cover and completing the interior pages. (Note: The directions and materials lists given are for making only one book. Multiply accordingly for the number of books you plan to make.)
- quick writing activities such as variations on the manipulative book and extension activities

Book Pages

Use card stock, construction paper, file folders, and other easy-to-find materials to create the books. Each book includes reproducible book pages for children to personalize with text and illustrations. Simply photocopy, cut out, and complete the reproducible book pages; then assemble the books as indicated in the directions. Some books include reproducible templates to create the cover. Books feature traditional songs, fun rhymes, and predictable text to support emergent readers.

Book Links

On page 48, you'll find recommended picture books for each bookmaking activity to enrich learning. Share the picture books before completing the manipulative books to build children's interest and background knowledge.

HOW TO MAKE MANIPULATIVE BOOKS

Getting Started

Before making books with students, gather the materials listed on the directions page. You might set up a writing center and keep a supply of bookmaking items organized in labeled plastic bins. Send home a letter to families requesting donations of supplies, such as fabric scraps, old magazines, ribbon, and so on.

Review the directions for a particular book project and determine which steps students will need assistance completing. Ask for parent volunteers to help in the bookmaking process.

Creating the Cover

Some of the books feature reproducible cover templates; others include easy directions for creating the cover. Follow the directions to create each cover, using materials such as construction paper and card stock. To save class time, cut the paper to the specified size in advance. Decorate the cover any way you'd like—or use the ideas listed in the directions.

Creating the Inside Pages

Photocopy the reproducible templates and cut them out. For a more colorful book, photocopy the templates onto different colors of paper. Review the directions for creating each book. Here are some additional suggestions:

- Before children begin writing, brainstorm possible responses to the prompts.

- Create charts of words and phrases for children to refer to when writing.

- Have children complete the art and text before binding the pages together.

- Have children write in pencil first, then check their work and have them trace their writing with thin marker.

Book-Making Basics

- ✳ lightweight card stock (available at office supply stores)
- ✳ copier paper
- ✳ construction paper
- ✳ file folders in assorted colors (available at office supply stores)
- ✳ tempera paint and brushes
- ✳ markers, crayons, and colored pencils
- ✳ safety scissors
- ✳ craft scissors (for adult use only)
- ✳ old magazines and catalogs
- ✳ stapler, glue, and tape
- ✳ hole punch
- ✳ yarn

Extra Goodies (optional)

- ✳ bright-colored copier paper or construction paper
- ✳ craft foam (plain and self-adhesive)
- ✳ white opaque markers (available at craft stores; great for drawing eyes or writing titles on dark paper)
- ✳ colorful dot stickers, labels, and name badges
- ✳ stickers
- ✳ rubber stamps and non-toxic washable dye ink pads
- ✳ glue gun (for adult use only)
- ✳ assorted art supplies such as ribbon, glitter, wiggly eyes, buttons, fake fur and fabric scraps, felt, and craft feathers

Binding the Books

Place the book pages in order and bind the book together as indicated in the directions. Please note that it is easier to complete the text and art before binding the pages together. Several of the books feature manipulatives that can be stored in resealable plastic attached to the covers. Have children use the little pieces to enhance, illustrate, or "act out" the text on each page. Your completed manipulative book is now ready to read and share!

Sharing the Books

Rereading text is an effective strategy for promoting fluency. Give children plenty of opportunities to interact with the text of each book before, during, and after making it. Here are some suggestions:

• Display the book's text in a pocket chart.

• Create a large collaborative class book or wall story with the book's text. Add children's illustrations.

• Place the completed manipulative books in your classroom library for independent reading.

• Read the completed books during small-group reading or guided reading time.

• Have children read their completed books with a classmate or upper-grade buddy.

• Have children store their completed books in empty cereal boxes that have been decorated.

• Send a note home to families offering suggestions for encouraging children to read their books, such as reading to family members or favorite stuffed animals, taking the books along to read in the dentist's waiting room, and having students glue a list to a book's inside back cover to keep track of all the people they've shared their book with.

Publishing Tips

• Adapt the directions and reproducibles to meet the needs of your students and curriculum.

• Invite children to make fun pointers to use as they read their finished books. Have them attach stickers or small objects to craft sticks. Glue or tape envelopes to the books and store the pointers inside.

• Use lightweight card stock instead of construction paper or poster board. It can be used in the copy machine, it's sturdy, and it's easier for little hands to cut than poster board.

• For instant repairs of errors that can't be erased, keep sheets of plain sticky labels handy. Just cover the error and keep on working!

• Invite children to add a "Meet the Author" page to the back cover.

The One and Only!

**Children create a book about themselves
with a self-portrait peeking over!**

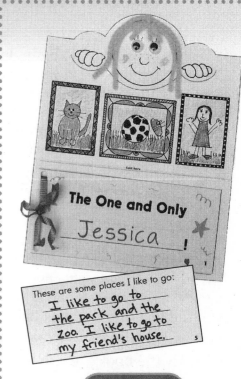

**Follow these steps to create a class book,
or help children create their own books.**

1. Photocopy page 9 on white construction paper or card stock. Cut out the template and cut along the line beneath the hands. (An adult should complete this step.) Fold up the page and tuck the bottom edge in the flap.

2. Open the book up and have children draw a self-portrait in the space between the hands. Invite them to add yarn hair, wiggly eyes, craft foam hats, and other fun details.

3. Instruct children to draw pictures in the three frames beneath their portrait. Brainstorm ideas such as family members, pets, friends, or special places. Or have children bring photographs from home with permission from families.

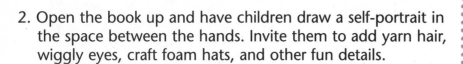

4. Photocopy pages 10 and 11 on white construction paper or copier paper. Cut out the pages.

5. Arrange the pages in order, place them in the box beneath the frames, and staple along the left side. Punch two holes and tie a ribbon through.

6. Have children write their name on page 1 and then respond to the writing prompts on each page. You might have children draw illustrations on the backs of the pages. If desired, add additional pages.

7. Fold the book closed. Have children write their name in the space beneath the flap. Encourage them to use large letters and add decorations with glitter, drawings, and so on. For added color, have children write their name on a colorful piece of construction paper and glue it in place.

MORE WRITING

- Use the templates to create a fold-up book with blank pages. Invite children to draw and write about family members, community or school helpers, friends, or favorite book characters.

MATERIALS
for 1 book

* cover template and book pages (pages 9–11)

* 8 1/2- by 11-inch white construction paper or card stock

* scissors

* crayons and markers

* art supplies such as yarn, wiggly eyes, craft foam, construction paper scraps, felt and fabric scraps, glitter, and stickers

* glue

* student photographs (optional)

* hole punch

* ribbon

fold here

The One and Only

_____!

1

This is what I look like:

_____

_____

_____

_____

2

These are the people in my family:

_____

_____

_____

_____

3

These are some things I like to do:

_____

_____

_____

_____

4

These are some places I like to go:

_____

_____

_____

_____

5

Here is more about the one and only me!

_____

_____

_____

_____

6

The Itsy Bitsy Spider

Children will have fun pushing a spider up the spout as they read and sing this favorite traditional song!

Follow these steps to create a class book, or help children create their own books.

1. Photocopy page 13 on orange paper. Copy pages 14–15 on white paper. Cut out the book pages.

2. Position the blue paper horizontally. Measure 4 inches from the left edge and fold the paper in along this line, as shown. Tape or staple the top and bottom of this fold to create a pocket. Measure 8 inches from the right edge of the paper and fold in along this line.

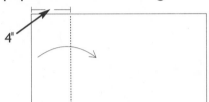 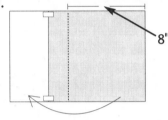

3. Glue the cover onto the front of the book. Either draw a spider on the cover or glue on a plastic spider. Place the "Little Miss Muffet" page in the pocket. As you collect other spider poems and pictures, store them in the pocket as well.

4. Fold a sheet of orange paper in half. Glue page 1 onto the front, pages 2 and 3 inside, and page 4 on the back.

5. Slide the spider ring onto a bendable straw. Bend the straw and tape it to the inside back cover, as shown in the photograph above.

6. Invite children to use crayons, markers, and construction paper scraps to finish the illustrations on each page. Suggest that they add a spider on each page, as well as rain on page 2 and a sun on page 3.

7. Insert the completed pages inside the cover. Punch two holes along the spine and bind the pages together with yarn or raffia. Show children how to move the spider up and down the "spout" as you read and sing the song.

MORE WRITING

- Add additional pages to the book. Invite children to write a new verse for the song. Encourage them to include a different kind of weather in their verse, such as wind or snow.

MATERIALS
for 1 book

* cover template and book pages (pages 13–15)

* 8 1/2- by 11-inch orange and white construction paper or card stock

* dark blue heavy construction paper or card stock, cut to 9 by 18 inches

* scissors

* transparent tape or stapler

* glue

* plastic spider (optional)

* crayons or markers

* bendable plastic straw

* plastic spider ring (available at some toy stores)

* construction paper scraps

* colorful yarn or raffia

Little Miss Muffet

Little Miss Muffet
sat on a tuffet,
eating her curds and whey.

Along came a spider
and sat down beside her,
and frightened Miss Muffet away!

The Itsy Bitsy Spider

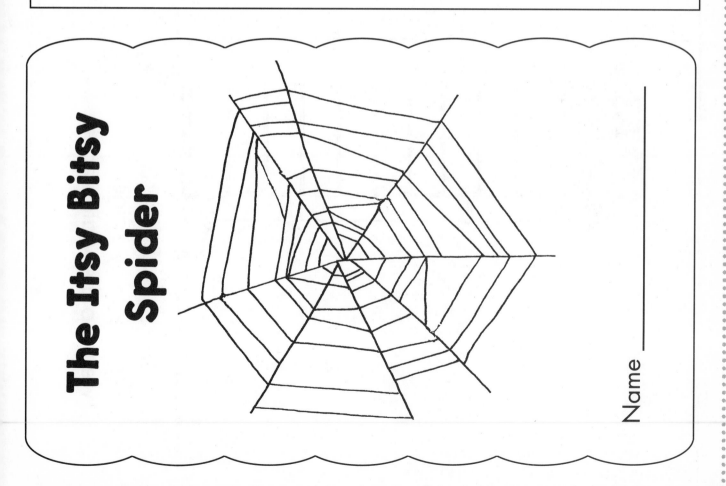

Name _____

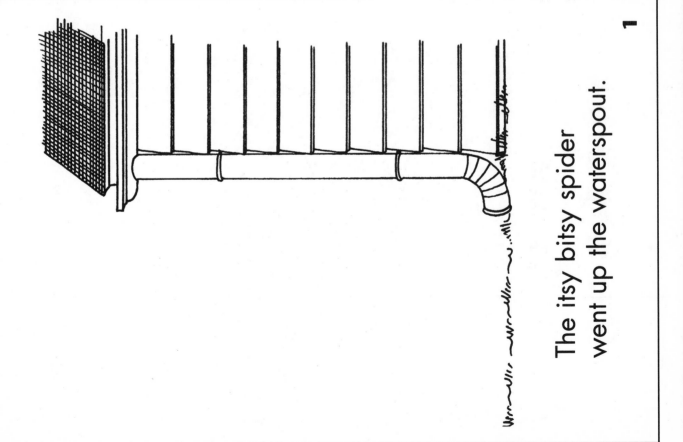

2

Down came the rain
and washed the spider out.

1

The itsy bitsy spider
went up the waterspout.

Super Manipulative Books   Scholastic Teaching Resources

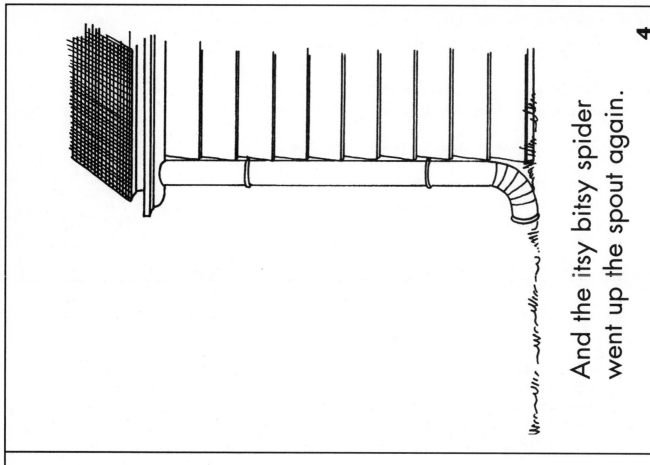

4

And the itsy bitsy spider
went up the spout again.

3

Out came the sun
and dried up all the rain.

My Book of Riddles

Children will have fun making, reading, and sharing these lift-the-flap riddle books.

Follow these steps to create a class book, or help children create their own books.

1. Fold the card stock in half to make the cover. Cut a sheet of construction paper in half to form two 8 1/2- by 5 1/2-inch pieces. Fold the pieces in half to make the interior book pages. Place the folded interior book pages inside the cover.

2. Punch two holes along the spine and bind the book with ribbon.

3. Write "My Book of Riddles" on a piece of colored paper and glue it to the cover. Draw colorful question marks.

4. Cut out the templates on page 17 along the solid lines. Position the large riddle template with the blank side facing up and flap 4 pointing right. Fold in flap 4, followed by 3, 2, and 1. Unfold the template and glue the square in the center. Repeat with pages 18 and 19.

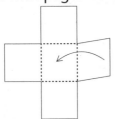

5. Fold up each template. Glue the templates onto the right-hand pages of the book. Glue the blank templates onto the last two pages.

6. Invite children to unfold the flaps as they read the riddles and guess the answer before lifting the last flap. Challenge them to write their own riddles with one clue on each blank flap and the answer in the center square. Have children exchange their completed books.

MORE WRITING

• Create riddle books for different topics of study—shapes, weather, seasons, habitats, and so on. Or make a class book featuring a riddle about each student. On the inside square, glue a student photo.

MATERIALS
for 1 book

* photocopies of riddle templates (pages 17–18)

* 2 photocopies of blank template (page 19)

* card stock cut to 8 1/2- by 5 1/2- inches (any color)

* 8 1/2- by 11-inch construction paper (different color than card stock)

* scissors

* hole punch

* ribbon

* markers

* construction paper scraps

* glue

One day, we went for a walk.

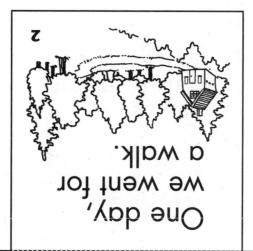

2

We found a girl asleep in bed. Who are we?

4

When we came back, our house was messed up!

3

We live in a house in the forest.

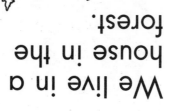

1

We are the 3 bears.

5

I am gray.
I have a tail.

1

I am in a book
about a girl
in red.

3

I am in a book
about 3 pigs.
Who am I?

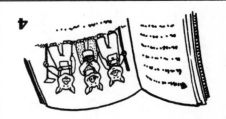

4

I live in the
woods.

2

I am the big
bad wolf!

5

1

Ɛ

ᔭ

2

5

What Time Is It?

Children move clock hands on a detachable clock to show various times as they read.

Follow these steps to create a class book, or help children create their own books.

1. Photocopy the clock and title pieces (page 21) on white card stock and cut them out. Carefully poke a hole through the clock and clock hands where indicated. Attach the hands to the clock using a brass fastener. (An adult should complete these steps.)

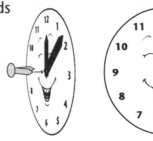

2. Fold a sheet of colored card stock in half to make a cover. Glue the title to the top of the book and the nameplate to the bottom. Use self-adhesive Velcro to attach the clock to the center of the cover.

3. To create sturdy book pages, fold two sheets of copier paper in half. Insert them in the cover, keeping the fold to the right. Staple along the left side.

4. Photocopy the interior book pages and cut them out. Glue them in order inside the book.

5. Invite children to complete the text. Have them choose a time to show both on the analog clock and the digital clock. Then have them write what they do at this time of day or night and draw a picture.

6. As you read the book, remove the clock from the cover and move the hands to show the time on each page. Simply attach the clock to the cover when finished!

MORE WRITING

• Distribute large index cards and have children write riddles to build math and time skills. On the front, have children write riddles such as "I put the cake in the oven at 2 o'clock. It must bake for 35 minutes. What time should I take the cake out?" Have them write the answers on the back.

MATERIALS
for 1 book

❋ cover template and book pages (pages 21–23)

❋ 8 1/2- by 11-inch card stock, any color and white

❋ 8 1/2- by 11-inch white copier paper

❋ brass fastener

❋ glue

❋ self-adhesive Velcro™ tape

❋ markers and crayons

❋ stapler

What Time Is It?

_____'s

Time Book

2

What time is it?

Can you tell the time?

It is _____

It is time to _____

1

It Is Time!

It is time to wake up.

It is time to eat.

It is time to clean up.

It is time to sleep.

What is my favorite time of day?

It is anytime I get to play!

4

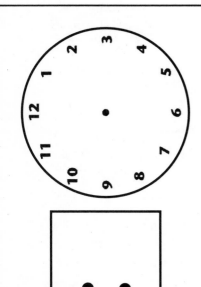

What time is it?

Can you tell the time?

It is _____

It is time to _____

3

What time is it?

Can you tell the time?

It is _____

It is time to _____

What Is in My Hand?

**Children explore the sense of touch
with this "hands-on" book.**

**Follow these steps to create a class book,
or help children create their own books.**

1. Make two photocopies of the cover template on card
   stock. Have children dip their hands in a contrasting color
   of finger paint and make a handprint on one cover. When
   the paint is dry, cut out the cover. Cut out the title and
   glue it onto the cover.

2. Make a photocopy of page 27. Cut out the poem and
   glue it onto the other photocopy of the cover. Use this
   as page 1 of the book.

3. Make several copies of page 26 on various colors of card
   stock and cut them out. Have children choose a small
   object to glue in the palm of each hand-shaped page.
   (If using a glue gun, complete this step for children.)

4. Invite children to finish the sentence and write words on
   the fingers that describe the object. Or, cut apart the
   words on page 27 and glue the appropriate words onto
   the fingers. You might also give children these words as
   a word bank for reference.

5. Arrange the pages in any order behind the cover and
   page 1. Staple them together along the left side. (Optional:
   Fold down the fingers and thumb on each page. As you
   read the book aloud, open the fingers one by one.)

MORE WRITING

- Use the hand template to make a collaborative book
  titled "Helping Hands." Have each student write and
  illustrate one page about a community or school helper.

- Make books about how "handy" students are. Use the
  templates to create a book with blank interior pages.
  Write the title "Our Hands Can" on the cover. On each
  page, have children write and illustrate one activity they
  can do with their hands, such as brushing their teeth or
  feeding their dog.

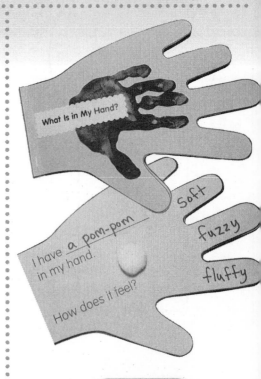

MATERIALS
for 1 book

* cover template and book pages
  (pages 25–27)

* 8 1/2- by 11-inch card stock
  (various colors)

* finger paint (various colors)

* scissors

* glue

* small, textured objects such as cotton
  balls, pom-poms, buttons, sandpaper
  scraps, corrugated cardboard, satin
  ribbon scraps, aquarium gravel, craft
  feathers, lima beans, straw or raffia,
  twigs, and seashells

* glue gun (optional, for adult use)

* stapler

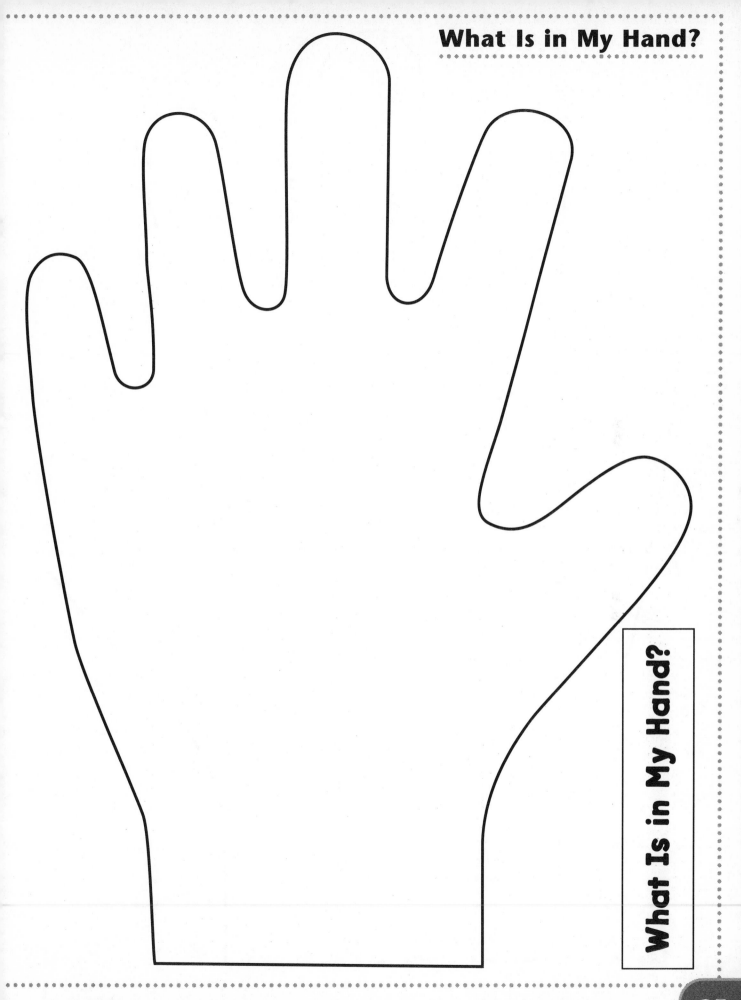

What Is in My Hand?

What Is in My Hand?

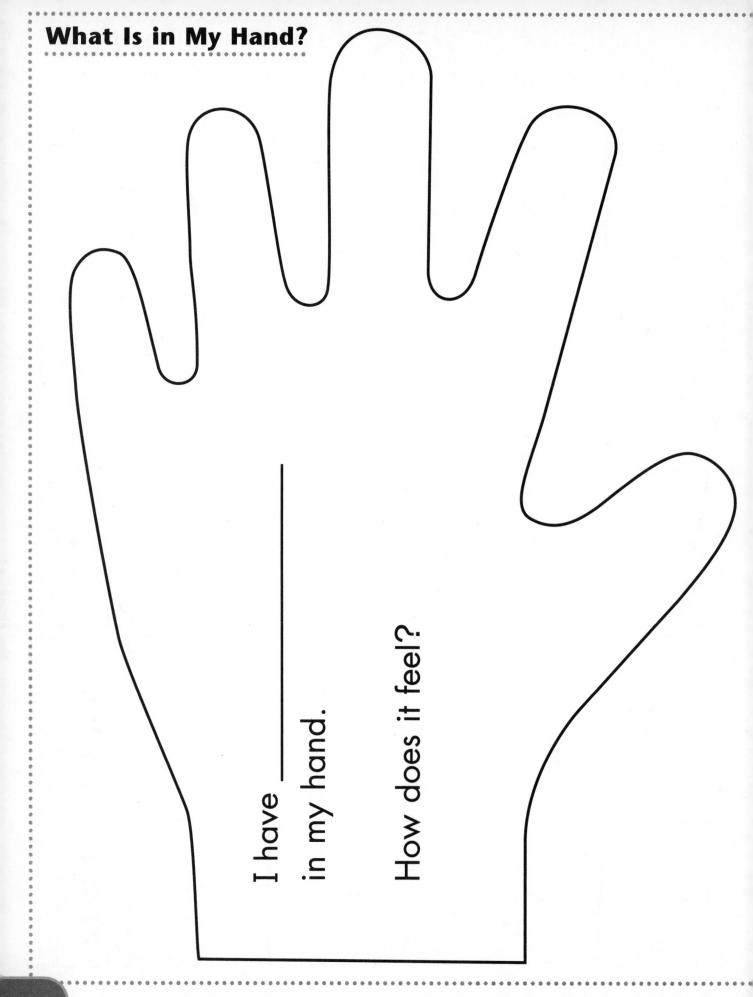

I have _____ in my hand.

How does it feel?

I have something in my hand.
What can it be?
Use your sense of touch,
and you will see!

bumpy	cold	fluffy
fuzzy	gooey	hard
itchy	prickly	rough
scratchy	smooth	soft
silky	slippery	sticky
mushy	warm	furry

Mary Wore Her Red Dress

Based on the traditional song, this book features a dress-up doll!

Follow these steps to create a class book, or help children create their own books.

1. For the book pages, make four copies of page 29 on white card stock. For a longer book, make additional copies.

2. Photocopy page 30 on white card stock and cut out the boxes. Glue one box to the bottom of each book page.

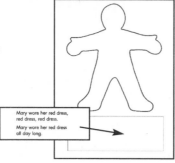

3. Photocopy page 31 on white card stock. Color and cut out the paper-doll clothes. Or trace the templates on colored foam paper. Attach small pieces of self-adhesive Velcro to the back of each piece of clothing. Then attach Velcro to the book pages where the clothes should be attached to the "paper dolls."

4. Write the title "Mary Wore Her Red Dress" on a small piece of white paper and glue it to the top of the red card stock. Place the book pages in the following order behind the cover: page 1—Mary, page 2—Henry, page 3—Peter, page 4—blank template. Staple the book together along the left side and staple a plastic bag to the cover. (Staple on the inside of the bag.) Store the clothing pieces in the bag.

5. Invite children to draw faces and hair on each paper doll. On the last page, have them fill in the blanks, following the pattern of the other pages. Tell students they can use their name, the name of a book character, or any other name. Then have them choose an article of clothing to feature on their page and write it on the lines.

6. As you read the book, "dress" each doll with the appropriate clothing. Attach a red dress to Mary, green sneakers to Henry, and so on. Then finish dressing each doll.

MORE WRITING

• Make four copies of page 30 and create a page for each of the other verses in the song: Sam, orange sweater; Hannah, pink sneakers; Leon, green shirt; Ashley, yellow hat.

MATERIALS
for 1 book

❋ book pages (pages 29–31)

❋ 8 1/2- by 11-inch white card stock

❋ 8 1/2- by 11-inch red card stock (or any other color)

❋ scissors

❋ glue

❋ craft foam scraps, various colors (optional)

❋ markers and crayons

❋ self-adhesive Velcro™ tape

❋ stapler

❋ small, resealable plastic bag

Note: To simplify this project, have children glue the articles of clothing onto the paper dolls, or simply use crayons or markers to draw clothing.

28

Mary wore her red dress,
red dress, red dress.

Mary wore her red dress
all day long.

1

Henry wore his green sneakers,
green sneakers, green sneakers.

Henry wore his green sneakers
all day long.

2

Peter wore his blue jeans,
blue jeans, blue jeans.

Peter wore his blue jeans
all day long.

3

_____ wore

_____

all day long.

4

Guess What Animal!

Enhance classroom animal studies with fun lift-the-flap riddle books.

Follow these steps to create a class book, or help children create their own books.

1. Photocopy pages 33 and 34. Have children finish the background art and color the animals with crayons, markers, or watercolor paints.

2. Photocopy page 35. (For a longer book, make additional copies.) Invite children to choose an animal and write their own clues along the left side of the page. Then have them draw a picture of the animal and write its name on the right side of the page. You might provide drawing books to help children with their illustrations.

3. Cut out each completed page and fold along the dotted line to hide the answer and illustration.

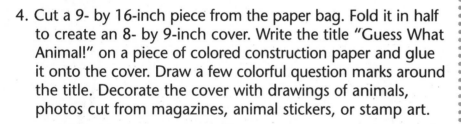

4. Cut a 9- by 16-inch piece from the paper bag. Fold it in half to create an 8- by 9-inch cover. Write the title "Guess What Animal!" on a piece of colored construction paper and glue it onto the cover. Draw a few colorful question marks around the title. Decorate the cover with drawings of animals, photos cut from magazines, animal stickers, or stamp art.

5. Insert the folded pages in the cover, punch two holes along the left side, and bind the book together with raffia or yarn.

6. Encourage children to share their books with a classmate. Have them read the clues, guess the animals, and then open the flaps to check their answers.

MORE WRITING

- Use the template on page 35 to create books about specific groups of animals. Categories could include farm, rain forest, desert, forest, ocean, and pets.

- Create a book with the same lift-the-flap format to write a collaborative class book of knock-knock jokes. Have each child contribute a page to the book, writing the joke on the left side and the answer on the right side. Encourage them to add humorous illustrations.

MATERIALS
for 1 book

* cover template and book pages (pages 33–35)

* watercolor paints and brushes

* markers and crayons

* instructional books on drawing animals (optional, see Book Links on page 48)

* large brown paper grocery bag

* construction paper scraps (various colors)

* glue

* old magazines featuring animal photos

* animal stickers, or animal stamps and non-toxic washable dye ink pads (optional)

* hole punch

* raffia or yarn

Guess what animal!

This animal lives in Africa.

It is covered with black or brown stripes

It is a grazing animal.

What animal is it?

It is _____.

Guess what animal!

This animal is the largest cat.

Each one has its own pattern of stripes.

It eats meat.

What animal is it?

It is _____.

Guess what animal!

What animal is it?

_____

_____

_____

_____

_____

_____

_____

It is _____.

Stone Soup

Serve up some "book soup," complete with vegetable manipulatives and a spoon!

Follow these steps to create a class book, or help children create their own books.

1. Photocopy the cover template on card stock. Sponge-paint the soup pot and let it dry before cutting it out. Add details with a black marker. As an alternative, color the pot with crayons or photocopy the template onto gray card stock.

2. To make the cover, write the title "_____'s Stone Soup" on a small piece of construction paper and glue it onto the black paper rectangle. Have children fill in the blank with their name.

3. Photocopy the book pages and vegetable manipulatives. For a longer book, make additional copies of page 38. Cut out the book pages, arrange them in order with the cover on top, and staple them to the bottom of the soup pot.

4. Color and cut out the vegetable manipulatives. For greater durability, glue them onto squares of construction paper. Store them in a plastic bag and staple it to the top of the soup pot. (Staple on the inside of the bag so it can easily be opened and closed.)

5. Invite children to take out the vegetable manipulatives and refer to them as they fill in the blanks on the book pages. When they have listed all the ingredients, have them return the manipulatives to the bag.

6. Glue a small stone to the plastic spoon and store the spoon in the bag. When reading the book, remove all the items from the bag. As you read each ingredient, find the corresponding manipulative, place it in the "pot," and stir everything up with the spoon. The spoon also doubles as a fun pointer!

MORE WRITING

• As a class, write a silly version of the Stone Soup story. Create manipulatives for unusual ingredients by drawing pictures and cutting out photos from magazines. Glue them onto construction paper scraps. Have fun coming up with wacky things to add to your soup! You might give your book titles such as *Robot Soup, Monster Stew, or Halloween Goulash.*

MATERIALS
for 1 book

* cover template, book pages, and vegetable manipulatives (pages 37–39)

* 8 1/2- by 11-inch white card stock

* gray tempera paint thinned with a little water

* small sponge

* black marker

* scissors

* construction paper scraps

* black construction paper, cut to 6 1/2 by 3 inches

* glue

* stapler

* small, resealable plastic bag

* plastic soup spoon

* small stone

Put in the _____.

Stir it up!

1

Put in the _____.

Stir it up!

2

Put in the _____.

Stir it up!

3

Put in the _____.

Stir it up!

4

Put in the _____.

Stir it up!

M-m-m-m! I made stone soup!

5

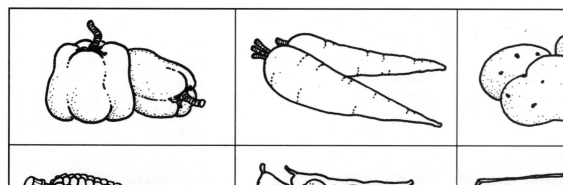

Frogs on a Log

Children practice subtraction with frog manipulatives as they read and sing this favorite traditional song.

Follow these steps to create a class book, or help children create their own books.

1. Photocopy and cut out the cover template. Place the lily pad on the fold of the file folder and trace the template. Cut out the traced shape, leaving the fold intact for the book's spine.

2. Glue wiggly eyes onto the frog. Draw a mouth, feet, and other details. Attach the dot stickers or paper circles and a bug sticker (optional). Write the title "Frogs on a Log."

3. Photocopy the book pages and frog manipulatives. Cut out the book pages, arrange them in order, and staple them to the inside back cover.

4. Color and cut out the frog manipulatives. For greater durability, glue them onto pieces of construction paper. For other fun manipulatives, use foam frog cutouts (available at craft stores), frog stickers, or small plastic frogs. Store the frogs in a plastic bag and staple it to the back cover. (Staple on the inside of the bag so it can easily be opened and closed.)

5. For each verse of the song, write a corresponding subtraction sentence on a craft stick. ($5 - 1 = 4$; $4 - 1 = 3$; $3 - 1 = 2$; $2 - 1 = 1$; $1 - 1 = 0$) Store the craft sticks in the bag.

6. Tell children to read the first page of the book and find the corresponding craft stick or "log." Show them how to place the frogs on the log and use them to show the subtraction problem. Then have children fill in the answer on the page and complete the rest of the book in the same way.

MORE WRITING

• After studying the life cycle of a frog, have children write and illustrate a nonfiction book about how a frog grows.

• Use the frog templates to create reading-response booklets for stories about frogs, such as the Frog and Toad series by Arnold Lobel or the Froggy series by Jonathan London.

MATERIALS
for 1 book

* cover template, book pages, and frog manipulatives (pages 41–43)

* green file folder

* scissors

* wiggly eyes

* glue

* black marker

* 6 light green dot stickers or small paper circles

* bug sticker (optional)

* stapler

* construction paper scraps

* small, resealable plastic bag

* 5 wide craft sticks

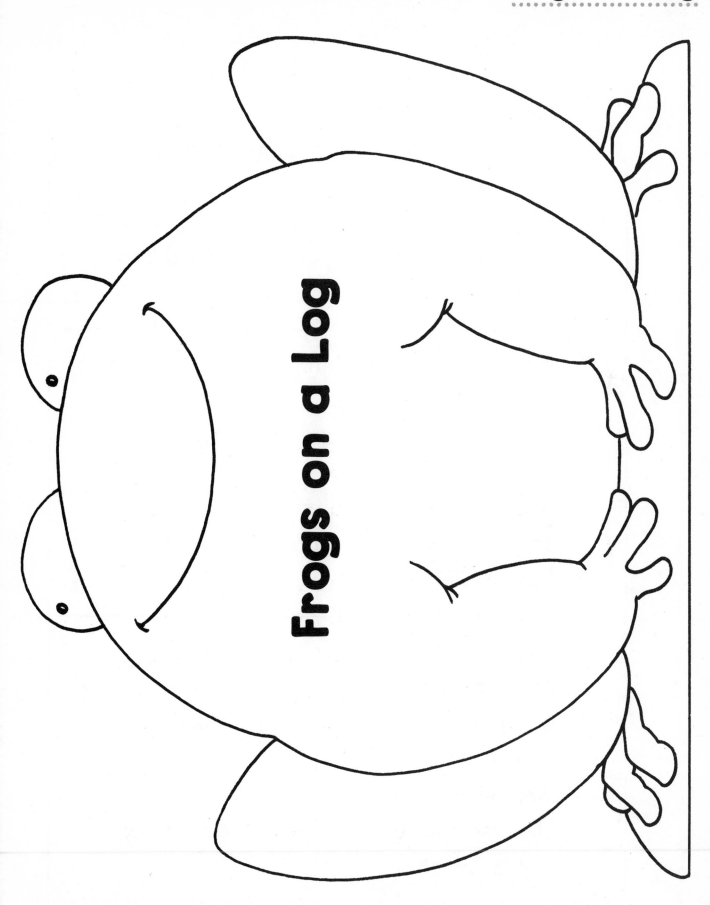

Frogs on a Log

Frogs on a Log

5 green and speckled frogs

sat on a speckled log,

eating the most delicious bugs. "Yum! Yum!"

1 jumped into the pool

where it was nice and cool.

Then there were _____ green speckled frogs.

"Glub! Glub!"

1

4 green and speckled frogs

sat on a speckled log,

eating the most delicious bugs. "Yum! Yum!"

1 jumped into the pool

where it was nice and cool.

Then there were _____ green speckled frogs.

"Glub! Glub!"

2

3 green and speckled frogs

sat on a speckled log,

eating the most delicious bugs. "Yum! Yum!"

1 jumped into the pool

where it was nice and cool.

Then there were _____ green speckled frogs.

"Glub! Glub!"

3

Super Manipulative Books   Scholastic Teaching Resources

2 green and speckled frogs

sat on a speckled log,

eating the most delicious bugs. "Yum! Yum!"

1 jumped into the pool

where it was nice and cool.

Then there was _____ green speckled frog.

"Glub! Glub!"

4

1 green and speckled frog

sat on a speckled log,

eating the most delicious bugs. "Yum! Yum!"

It jumped into the pool

where it was nice and cool.

Then there were no green speckled frogs.

"Glub! Glub!"

5

How a Butterfly Grows

This eye-catching accordion book features a colorful clip-on butterfly.

Follow these steps to create a class book, or help children create their own books.

1. Photocopy the cover and book pages onto light-colored paper. Cut out the pages.

2. Fold the construction paper in half lengthwise. Fold it into four equal sections, then refold along the creases like an accordion.

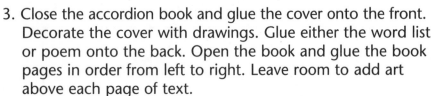

3. Close the accordion book and glue the cover onto the front. Decorate the cover with drawings. Glue either the word list or poem onto the back. Open the book and glue the book pages in order from left to right. Leave room to add art above each page of text.

4. Paint the pasta pieces as follows: miniature pasta or popcorn kernel—white (egg), spiral pasta—yellow and black stripes (caterpillar), shell pasta—green (chrysalis), bow tie pasta—orange (butterfly). Allow the paint to dry. Twist a 3-inch piece of pipe cleaner around the center of the bow tie pasta to form two antennae.

5. Cut three 3-inch green paper leaves. Then decorate each book page as follows:
   - Page 1: Attach a leaf. Glue the "egg" onto the leaf.
   - Page 2: Attach a leaf. Glue the "caterpillar" to the leaf.
   - Page 3: Attach a leaf. Glue the "chrysalis" so it looks like it's hanging from the underside of the leaf.
   - Page 4: Attach a flower made from construction paper scraps. Glue the butterfly on or above the flower.

6. Pinch the tissue paper in the center to create two wings. Open the clothespin and glue the wings inside. Twist the 5-inch pipe cleaner in the center to make two antennae. Open the clothespin and glue it inside. (An adult should complete these steps.) Glue the pom-poms onto one side of the clothespin. Glue on wiggly eyes and clip the butterfly onto your book.

MORE WRITING

- Make accordion books to show the life cycles of other animals, such as chickens or frogs.

MATERIALS
for 1 book

- cover template and book pages (pages 45–47)
- scissors
- 12- by 18-inch dark blue construction paper
- glue
- construction paper scraps
- miniature pasta or popcorn kernel
- spiral pasta, shell pasta (approximately 1 inch), bow tie pasta
- white, yellow, black, green, and orange tempera paint and small brush
- thin pipe cleaner, cut into a 3-inch piece with sharp ends folded in
- green construction paper
- 3- by 6-inch colored tissue paper
- spring-type clothespin
- 5 pom-poms, 1/2 inch wide
- regular pipe cleaner, cut into a 5-inch piece with sharp ends folded in
- 2 small wiggly eyes

Super Manipulative Books   Scholastic Teaching Resources

How a
Butterfly
Grows

by _____

A little egg sits on a leaf.
Inside a little critter sleeps.

1

A caterpillar hatches out.
It munches leaves and
crawls about.

2

Then it changes
shape and hides.

3

Look!
I see a butterfly!

4

Science Words

Egg

Caterpillar

Chrysalis

Butterfly

Butterfly Garden

Flutter, flutter! What do you see?

Eight bright butterflies flying free!

It would be nice if they would stay—

But flutter, flutter, six sail away.

Then two butterflies are left to play.

—Liza Charlesworth

BOOK LINKS

Share these read-alouds to build children's
interest, vocabulary, and background knowledge.

The One and Only!
All by Myself by Mercer
Mayer (Golden, 2001)
Little Critter is proud of what
he can accomplish on his own.

Things I Like by Anthony
Browne (Knopf, 1989)
A chimp shares some of his
favorite activities.

The Itsy Bitsy Spider
The Itsy Bitsy Spider by Iza Trapani
(Whispering Coyote Press, 1993)
Various obstacles interfere with
the little spider as she sets out
to climb a tree and spin a web.

Spider on the Floor by Bill Russell
(Crown, 1993)
This playful song describes the
unusual things a spider catches
in its web as it climbs a lady.

My Book of Riddles
ABC Animal Riddles by Susan
Joyce (Peel Productions, 1999)
Readers answer rhyming riddles
about mystery animals for every
letter of the alphabet.

Who Am I? Hello Reader by Nancy
Christensen (Scholastic, 1993)
Animals give rhyming clues
about their identities.

What Time Is It?
The Completed Hickory Dickory Dock
by Jim Aylesworth (Atheneum, 1990)
The mouse's adventures continue
through each hour.

Monster Math School Hello Math
Reader by Grace Maccarone
(Scholastic, 1998)
Readers learn about time as they
follow twelve monsters through
their school day.

What Is in My Hand?
Is It Rough? Is It Smooth? Is It Shiny?
by Tana Hoban (Greenwillow, 1984)
A wordless book showcases various
objects in colorful photographs.
How many ways can students
describe the pictures?

Mary Wore Her Red Dress
Jesse Bear, What Will You Wear?
by Nancy White Carlstrom
(Macmillan, 1986)
Rhyming text tells about
Jesse deciding what to wear
throughout the day.

*Mary Wore Her Red Dress and
Henry Wore His Green Sneakers*
by Merle Peak (Clarion, 1985)
Katy Bear's friends arrive at her
birthday party in outfits of
all colors. Includes an audio
tape of the song.

Guess What Animal!
I Can Draw Animals by Ray
Gibson (Sagebrush Education
Resources, 1998)
Simple step-by-step instructions
show how to draw a variety
of animals.

My Visit to the Zoo by Aliki
(HarperCollins, 1997)
Take an informative visit to a
zoo that features animals in
natural habitats.

Who Says Moo? by Ruth Young
(Viking, 1994)
Rhyming animal riddles provide
clues about each creature's
characteristics.

Stone Soup
Growing Vegetable Soup by Lois
Ehlert (Brace Jovanovich, 1987)
Learn how seeds in the garden
eventually lead to soup in a pot.

Monkey Soup by Louis Sachar
(Knopf, 1992)
A concerned child combines
unusual ingredients to create
a healing soup for her father.

Stone Soup retold by Heather Forest
(August House LittleFolk, 1998)
Two travelers teach the townspeople
that the secret ingredient in stone
soup is sharing.

Frogs on a Log
The Frog Alphabet Book by Jerry
Pallotta (Charlesbridge, 1990)
This colorful alphabet book features
fascinating amphibians from *A* to *Z*.

Ultimate Kids Song Collection
(Madacy Records, 2000)
This collection of three CDs
includes "Five Little Speckled Frogs"
as well as 100 other favorite songs.
Visit **www.amazon.com** to listen
to the song.

How a Butterfly Grows
I'm a Caterpillar Hello Reader by
Jean Marzollo (Scholastic, 1997)
Simple text describes the life
cycle of a caterpillar.

Where Butterflies Grow by
Joanna Ryder (Lodestar, 1989)
Experience the life cycle of a
butterfly from the butterfly's
perspective.